P9-CMK-343

For Stuart, Riley, and Charlie
— Shona Innes

For my ever best seesaw friend, Dorka
— Írisz Agócs

First North American edition published in 2014 by Barron's Educational Series, Inc.

Text copyright © Shona Innes, 2014
Illustrations copyright © Írisz Agócs, 2014
Copyright © The Five Mile Press, 2014

*All inquiries should be addressed to:*
Barron's Educational Series, Inc.
250 Wireless Boulevard
Hauppauge, New York 11788
**www.barronseduc.com**

ISBN: 978-0-7641-6748-5
Library of Congress Control Number: 2014932022

Date of manufacture: May 2014
Manufactured by: Waiman Book Binding (China) Ltd, Kowloon, Hong Kong, China

Printed in China

9 8 7 6 5 4 3 2 1

# FRIENDSHIP Is Like a Seesaw

Shona Innes * Irisz Agócs

BARRON'S

Friendships are funny and precious things.
Friendships come in many shapes and sizes.

Friendships are built by the way
we get along with friends.

Friends can be old or new.
A good friendship is a very
special thing to have.

Good friends agree on the rules.

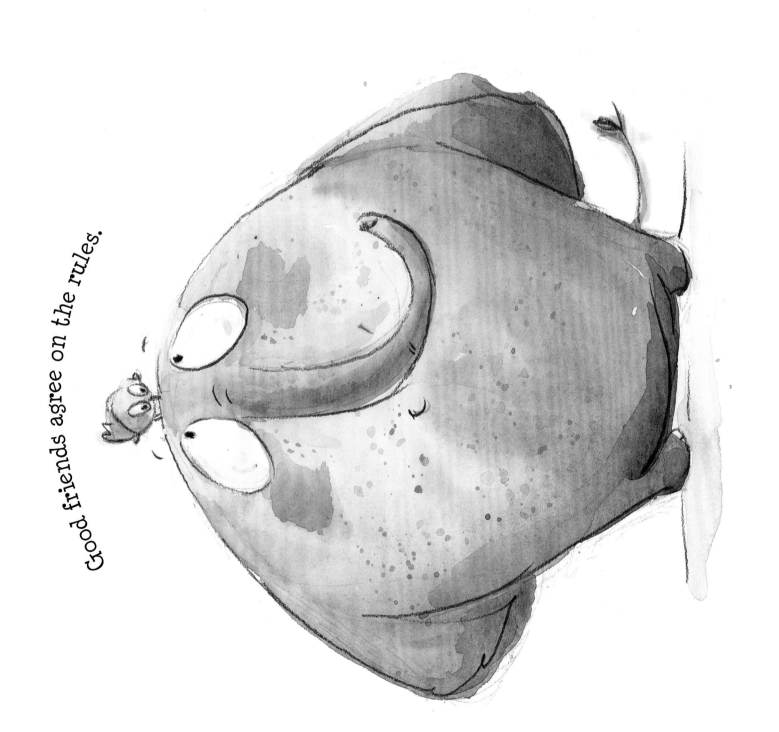

They do nice things for each other,
they are kind, and they help when
one is feeling down.

Good friends take turns,
share, and have fun together as they play.

Sometimes friendship can be a little bit like a seesaw. When friends play on a seesaw, one side goes up, and the other side goes down.

When a seesaw is even on both sides, it is balanced.

And when one side goes down, the other side of the seesaw goes up.

Friendship is like a seesaw.

Sometimes you might feel up in the air

when your friend feels low.

Other times, you might feel down when your friend is up.

When a friendship is even on both sides, it is balanced.

When things are balanced,
both friends feel happy.

Sometimes a friendship can get out of balance
if one friend is feeling troubled or low.

It might be out of balance because there is a problem that needs fixing.

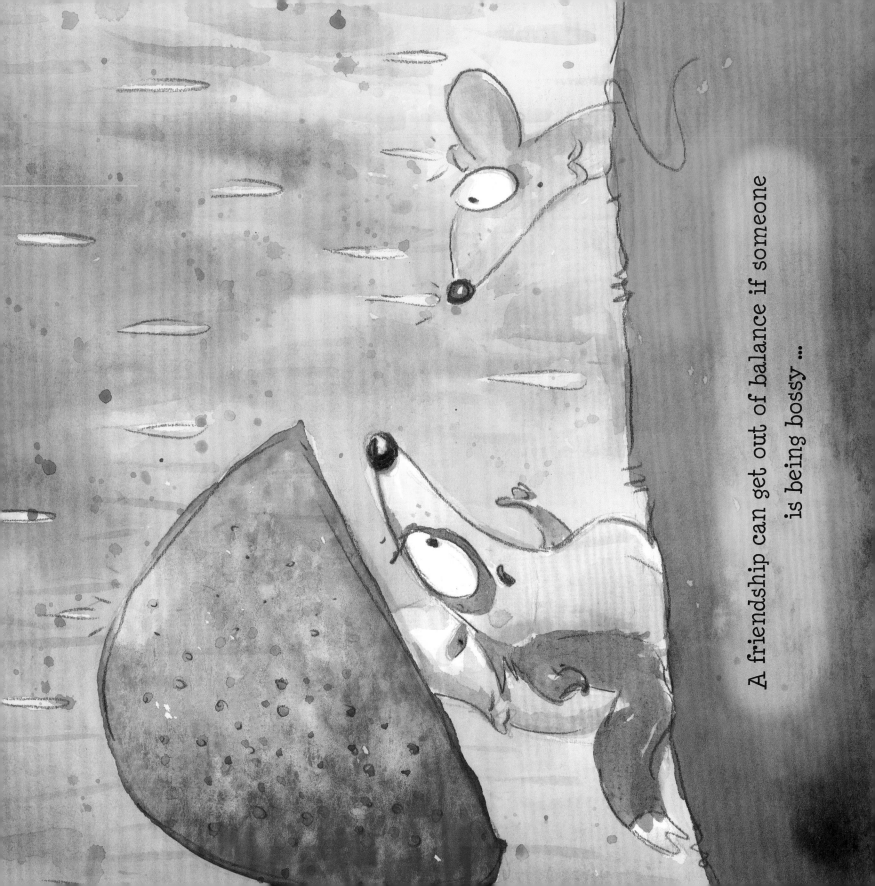

A friendship can get out of balance if someone is being bossy ...

...or if someone is being sulky.

Sometimes, instead of the friendship feeling good, you might feel bad about the friendship feeling good.

Friends might say or do hurtful things,
or leave you out of the fun.

When a friendship is uneven and troubled,
you might feel very sad or angry.

But there are things you can do to rebalance and fix the friendship.

You can tell your friend that you are not happy and see if you can work it out together.

Sometimes we might need to stop and check
if our own friendship skills are working.

Sometimes, we might even need to take
a break from a friend for a while.

It can really hurt when a troubled friend makes you feel bad. You might want to hurt him back, but that will only make things worse. Things will still be out of balance.

Instead, you can do lots of things that will make you feel better.

You can do nice things for other people, or play with other friends,

or enjoy some quiet time by yourself doing the things that you love to do.

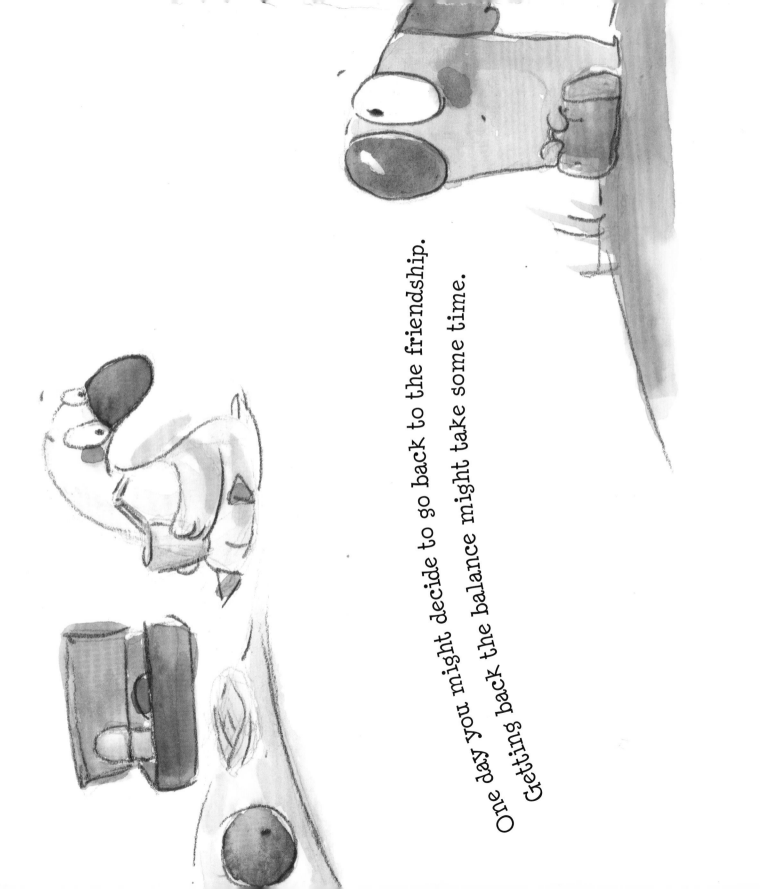

One day you might decide to go back to the friendship.
Getting back the balance might take some time.

And maybe even laugh about the troubles you had.

But when things are even again, you can play and be happy together.